Un-Sight/ Un-Sound
(delirium X.)

UN-SIGHT/ UN-SOUND
(DELIRIUM X.)

M

gnOme

gnOme books
gnomebooks.wordpress.com

Please address inquiries to:
gnomebooks@gmail.com

Cover image source: Mabel Loomis Todd, *Total Eclipses of
the Sun* (Boston: Roberts Brothers, 1894), 3 [public
domain].

ISBN-13: 978-0692334799.
ISBN-10: 0692334793.

(...the senseless attention, analogous to the fear that intoxication can be, to the intoxication that fear can be...)

...not a line where, like the morning dew in the sunshine, the sweetness of anguish does not come into play...

...I really ought to...
...but I want to wipe out my footprints...

— Georges Bataille

CONTENTS

I

DELIRIUM X.

1...

...in stun light of bled ember embark viscid endless

...marked trace of scar scar's out-breath of reach emptier than

...dead spark of wound collapse headless viper taste attrition

...zero foreign else passage absent absenteeism

...shadow lock a slashed throat a severed artery rope mark indent the teeth the

...eye foreign as of dead I lapsing here or there another eye of glass or other than

.../I really out to/

...subtle low black vibrate of toxic blood its seals unbroken

...jackal tryst here or there another's abort another's laughter long corridors of abnegation negation

...I lies it cannot recollect [it] razor slash dreaming yet of something other than

...the *yes* of wiping out one's footsteps it matters not a

...eye lapse and the bitten flesh the reek the answering of

...drawing across the curtains in roomscape made of flesh bones scuttling for the silence

...desire desire dread-dread desire dread dread desire

...ice petals as if to say that once no emptily

...subtle as as of till of ever the ongoing of till until

...emblem of seared meat tracing the body broken the fingers severed

...opens up the wound of discharge of rotten stone the acrid traces of which designed by

...closing the cataract fist within the occult wound of bloodless lifeless ever having been

...children's toys/ as if to say that/ sings *Mar Di Gras*

...slices open envelope with bone knife in bloodstained hand

...was once it says henceforth there /*I really ought to*/

...the sands' in-dreaming they are of the foreign else

...the eye closes divides divides nothing conquered nothing...

2...

...*'you must eat of it,'* (it says)

...of the excreta-smeared eye the questions ask breathless as if to forage vacant absolute

...subtle as a snapped jaw bone emptier than emptied out a theatre of cardboard cut-outs the serrated promise of

...here or there a lung locked suitcase full of carrion

...given unto the taste of it harking back unto claims none it devours driven ecstasy

...dry them

...shadow what what

...shadow yes or no as if unto as if of drift will what wind in

...sky sky of the outstretched arm of X.

...blood trance of the Baconesque abort the canvas slashed across its seals unbroken by the silence of

...damage endless damage what what damage else there

....*(the   season's devour)*

...excess of blind light the demarcations of distemper

...bled again as if from lack loss lapse of the sky a brow drenched in bitter sweat

...yet colourless yet/ scald/ mocked once I lies that it could yet be alive or dead given the yes or no the redemptive of the none spread-speech soundless spaces

...here or there a bathtub full of bones wrenched from the approximate light

...(dry them

...no-not the heart)...

...eats the meat of it it is not said it is of the final asking

...(*beneath the denuded feet of a beautiful woman the floor writhes in a consumptive tragedy*)

...tells once then asked

...walls wombs of teeth the tooth's snare the begun spoke once haven from out of shadow build collapse deathly as

...(closes the door)

...in tragedia

...(curtains close)

3...

...indelible shadow bone light of a circus dreaming until foreign X./ lapse into or out of vacant as of eye's definite disappearance

...trades detritus of light bloodless fission collapse subtle as of lock the teeth a-grind semblant what semblance

...ashen smiles of the dislocate of skin terse redeem wall warp of psychotic atrophic

...*vision impaired by the uncertainty of a future*

...blind children unearthed circuit ache what of it the aching flesh blank light bile of the unshod cadaver

...written writ stone blind

...(*quiet tonight, not a sound, as if the earth were... uninhabited*)

...knock-knock astray so there it goes flows unto latrine phallus a dead white vacant socket pulse of

..."at the beginning I..."

...(in the beginning, 'I')

...circus light of bone incurious spasm of dead in in-dreaming else of what matter it is said as if to say

...(*the camera is the eye of a cruising vulture flying over an area of scrub, rubble and unfinished buildings on the outskirts of...*)

...no nothing nowhere of left or right or breath escapes

...voice no longer rapture closed fist slash breath lack endless collapse vicious

...vortices phlegm soundless a returning echo distant light bled fathom

...(sounds as if to/ eviscerated/ not a)...

...a returning echo bled distant light no longer as if to

...fingers severed to taste the black milk of sky's abandon

...cut teeth nausea of the given bones as

...fucks one then the other then one it fucks the other one

...excessive blindness a candle slashed out

...it has never burned so brightly the blue flame of the flesh abounding/ ... / drift

...it cannot

...speechless for all given time what time of which to be given unknown as if it/ where

...(end quote)

4...

I'm hungry for blood
hungry for bloody earth
hungry for fish hungry for rage
hungry for filth hungry for cold
                    — GEORGES BATAILLE

...fag-end of death

...eclipse of violent meat foreign spasm clotted blood clot

...dense as shit the light-break stun of absolute

...pissoir of irredeemable loveless state the exposed thorns of

...black metallic eye severance clear cut a window shattered

...eye perceives none dissolve dissolved absenteeism

...final ice of breath unspun belong to not of this earthen final erupt spinal ask shadow's vertebrae

...spinning top of exhumed configurative null void in nihilo

...zeroed out cast upon bile of the inflexed skull amphetamine

...hungry for blood hungry for...*annihilation*

...bodies meld in a kaleidoscope of intricate colours their skins vibrate a scent of musk and vibrant sex

...blood cold fish filth hunger for earth for absence

...in the scum of the dark the restless membrane seeks seek lest you falter prayers from the deep bound and gagged a flourish of unspeaking death-dreams

...the wounds lay open birthing eye eye still blind

...stillness of the corrupt heart its seals unbroken fathom scuttle of seek lest you or other than or of/ violet

...'I' can hear the blades sharpening in the night birthed atrophic silences from out of spasm again murmuring of frugal/ ashen

...the words drift away afar there is no passage from state till grace in-between the once of lack till breach the barb in the flesh

...zone white

...the eye upturned it has no shadow

...hungry for...

...ice fragmented dissipation not a trace

...'I' has long ceased to be

...slowly the shadow's inhale of breath as time disposes

5...

> '...*taken by the maggots for what they are.*'
> — SAMUEL BECKETT

...light's rot in amber distances claimed as the tongue torn out spat out whatever the

...no distance ever unto

...rub shit into the wound

...ice-pick in desolate heart your Lord your worship

...(*these are your walls/ they are for all time*)

...never has a man painted silence like de Chirico

...'this is the room, the start of it all'*

...im[possible] traces of she of which 'I' has not yet died nor

...out from out of which end world an end of smeared in cancerous blood

...child sting distances only left to trace wandering convulsive in black-light/ echo-echo/ lacking the pulse of

...no nothing ever

...*drag up thy cross and walk*

...scattered bones and teeth line pathways poignant burnished leather upon bone snap

...the grind of the machine spitting spumes of none and the given a taste for obsolete

...exhalations of opiate smoke and the reek of tear's indent upon as the flesh rots from Krokodil innards

...night ever as if ever was as if and yet or of as if it other than or of

...'I open in myself a false theatre...'**

...'A disgrace that sickens me...'**

...peels away the skin away from the flesh a smear of teeth catches a glint of radioactive light

...trades flesh for flesh

...desolate the zero eye unceasing

...words

...nothing

*(Ian Curtis)

**(Georges Bataille)

6...

For once
and in the light of a body flayed
in a pigsty of eagles
the thief of fire will swallow himself
his liver

      — GHERASIM LUCA

...of the eye's extract it cannot detraced no it not a of the eye's detract it cannot be detraced

...feel of the shotgun laughter of the sun's caress bled out from exile unto exodus dead sands broken hieroglyphs

...locked bone nothing severed ever nothing none of nothing less than none that is or of the naught said without

...black stone blood of exigent need steel bled mask bitter of the compel endless to delve

...emblems of shadowed veins collective absence dry rot in a given palm stigmata-excrement/ devoured

...bleeds word from words stunt echo-pageant of reverb casting the cards to the open winds cares not for the distance travailed

...utter dark wind breathe of occult spasm heart minced spasm grief of ever having stepped bone laughter else or

...it cannot not once thrice splice of the eye's absurd lock give or take or take never having forgotten given taken

...these are the dead lands these are the cactus lands vacant space the echoing memory of children's laughter

...the sky smeared across by wormed fingers trace of ejaculate a distant desert of feel scum dead alack breathing in the midst the harvest/ erase/ commence

...'I' aches disappears end of foreign no not of the reek of

...from out of roomscape destitute blessed rabidous jaws taut in or of from the beginning less or for of butchery

...sings no not of skinned the sings not the eye of it marrow shadow breathe again as if inhales exhales what matter

...it closes the door upon footprints erased by the winds

...*we all fall down*

...we/ all/ fall/ down

...an open grave an open wound to penetrate

...say goodbye say farewell until unto/ unspoken

7...

> ...'We are all agnostics, transvestites of art
> or of sex. None of us has either aesthetic or
> sexual convictions any longer – yet we
> profess to have them...A postmodern
> pornography, if you will, where sexuality is
> lost in the theatrical excess of ambiguity.'
>   — JEAN BAUDRILLARD

...a lubricious scar opened in the head of a dead young woman lain out upon an operating table a scattering of medical instruments upon cold metallic sheen

...blind light forces the corpus to exfoliate

...a severed breast a severed cock and the raw red ash of a bloodless wound

...silver the glint is fucking the eye sockets of desire a taste of ashes the fingers glued to the keys of cerebral flesh by viscous blood and cum

...transvesticidal zero point from out which the simulation expands collective dead spasm of blind shit seethe of the unbecoming penetrative exodus

...what loss what love what funeral pyre sun light what of

...a noose of degenerative conceptualisations swings like a broken tooth hanging from a still-born nerve tint approximating

...words spoken collect the dust not a sound absence of purity dead speech and the declouded absence of falling leaves carved from bone the

...prayers from the deep to non-speech as if from out of till end and then over and again till shadow less ever less

...cigarette smoke devours the lung's impulse to retract hardened sickly devours the impulse

...(said aside...)

...the ghost limbs of amputee nothingness extracted fingernails

...(with a subtle clip here or there we clip a segment say a fingertip a toe extract a tooth make a stitch futile work much like plumbing really as if to unclog)

...*everything is pornography pornography is everything*

...exotic laughter echoes from the corridors

..."ah, slide it across and be done with it..."

...utensils washed clean/ bereft

...in the tray the final eye's removal/ I/ fingers inserted into

...the rains fall heavily trace across the glass like translucent veins closing the eyelids nothing has happened no nor will in the excessive lack of intent

"*...and the worst are filled with passionate intensity*"*

*(W.B Yeats)

8...

Instead of a mouth and an anus to get out of order why not have an all-purpose hole to eat and eliminate? We could seal up nose and mouth, fill the stomach, make an air hole direct into the lungs where it should have been in the first place.
— WILLIAM S. BURROUGHS

...anal teeth surrogate the advocacy of ache + 1 dissolve + naught

...eliminate the source it will not rescind blackened flesh discolourisation of sky bleed of

...the shit will arise to the inner chamber of the gaping wound of mouth open and close the cock slides in the tongue slides out into the cunt

...however how and ever exhales the blind mock dense ashen corrupt file zero +

...eliminate the product and there is the cunt vacancy the anal vacancy cured by birth and shit

...cycle death hollow breath

...the bruised veins of absent gain

...pin-prick teeth shattered shadow silhouette upon a whitewashed wall broken unsealed its seals forgotten emblems

..."...where it should have been in the first place."

...seal the wind drag up the flesh the meat what have you the erect cock as if to unsheathe the drown of collective absolute disarm expulsion

...dead less or more than once

...out of which the cruciform phallus in juggernaut drill
between the thighs impermanence governed by

...(as if to say...)

...stitch shut the wounds

...shit/ birth/ one or the other pretty much the same

9...

> *I've always been very moved by pictures about slaughter- houses and meat, and to me they belong very much to the whole thing of Crucifixion...Of course, we are meat, we are potential carcasses. If I go into a butcher shop I always think it surprising that I wasn't there instead of the animal.*
> — FRANCIS BACON

...abattoir love hence or viewed in the mirror of the spoon's reflect a syringe tarnish of the collective ice blood wilted given just a taste

...injected somnolence of an unseen sky perfectly formed the outstretched arms of babes cometh the hour the night the day

...birthed lapse of the orificial opening insert here extract deSadean excavation absolution extinction but for an hour or less or of the given or other

...the bulb weight of in-dreaming splayed speech: flesh hangs from the bones the shard revealed it follows through the bled sun of design a meat hook stylus

...colours acrid a foreign spell

...dreamed less than of in spiral flesh not of yet of in circus dreamed settled in loveless abattoir alone

...'I' skys with its little eye the bulk of it repressed innards shifting of the gravity's placement a revolution with without answer a blank death a subtle discourse

...carcass kisses to become the light peals an arena of

acrid colour a taste of foreign light shimmer-glimmer-taste in the mouth in the gouge of the mouth of stale ashes kisses carcass benevolence

...cylindrical discharge elected to this

...nothing spoken of it no not a word of what

...meat

...and of the all that shimmers is not gold glimmers yet is of the blood's final light unspeaking speechless utterances

...the carnival skeleton reveals nothing unless strip-skinned unless the orifices of which what once created dense as shit the very shit that conquers reduces/ (context)

...cruciformed against a diseased sky that reveals the discolourisation of the eye that perceives

...(enters socket once more)

...the skin binds the locus

...benign against unsung walls a colossus to taste shocks none utter shock crimson

...raw taste of blood in the mouth

...(*carnivale*)

...(*carnivale*)

...utter dark of the surround

10...

> *all I hear leave out more leave out all hear*
> *no more lie there in my arms the ancient*
> *world without end me we're talking of me*
> *without end that buries all mankind to the*
> *last cunt they'd be good moments in the dark*
> *the mud hearing nothing saying nothing*
> *capable of nothing nothing*
>
> — SAMUEL BECKETT

...not an ounce not a.../ beginning overly begun

...too far the night for dreaming of the head the swallowing of it spent force absentee laughter burning up the surplus light

...itches to be gone done vacant teeth to pare away in the meantime

...ocular dead roving as if to say of the bleed as if to say roving in the abattoir ditches green as acrid grasses of the membrane to disavow

...nothing saying

...ancient the words they come to the fore there is no room for dry tears in the mercury blood

...a piss-frenzy of the absurd catascope in roomscape or was it of the before or after gleaming some sunlight glistening in the ejaculative cum breath mark it well

...nothing nothing no shears no running with scissors run with scissors unto opening up the graven spill it out lapse sleep nestling the bone

...dousing the flame from out of having begun nowhere

ending nowhere dreaming of the less than before cleft
savoured unsung benign

...clap hands

...foraging footsteps down long corridors of breath

...yet never having left the room a simple -what- no
nothing less or more simple than occult excavation

...a guillotine brace feels for the mark at the throat
kisses the silence ever more than before semblant night

...night carouses the

...echoes echo echoing

...a smeared image in the glass

...the glass reveals nothing/ nothing

...passage passage in the intestinal tract

...words clear the sheet the sheet ablaze here now or for
what or of the hereafter not a...[SOUND]

...never having been/ or

11...

...(*says the naught*)

...axial rent none of bask speech retraced expelled shattered cast as of seed to the blood-streaked winds

...long streak of given desire meat circus savoured spent till absolute eradicate but for momentum cast of dice of the plateau reached given of

...slow burst of flowerings in the eyes of the beheld what then or next till dreamed of foreign in the execution of it/ (falsity)

...succour no/ asking of till fortitude/ a

...deals deathcards from out of emblem isolated the pulse returns from the none ever to the else to become

...isolated the pulse disavows locks its teeth around the escaping sign of night

...crystallisation none of haven bleached surrogate rent none of bask harvest of as of absolute

...mocks the furtive as if it had presence none spoken of the nothing of must be accepted as '*some thing other*'

...all the while in bitter sun's damage in bitter son's lessening too old for the lash the breaking pulse disregards disregard

...'I' aches in the shadowed corners of every room that ever spread its cunt skinned the walls awaken the crest of

...there is laughter the laughter of alone in the meat

emblems of bind-bound fixative cum strike a match

…'I' remembers

…merely the drowning out the ferocity of sound that is the conscious of drawing breath aloud it speaks of future else beyond else none

…what speaks of what

…ice bind

…the none's haven/ the absence's reside

12...

The empty room begins to howl
And I myself empty
Without a single bone

Turn into a hundredfold
Echo of howling

And echo echo
Echo

— VASKO POPA

...turns into echo of howling turns into a hundredfold of bitten snare white blood corpuscle itch screams silence

...excavates the skull of none draught in shadow vent collapse broken valves emptied valves of

...speech driven from the locked ice of frozen amber welts close of fist as of time divulged rent rixt eye non-said it turns away

...it turns to nothing never once having pregnant with gutter stench reek of the benign light rotting in the cavities the epi-centres

...such and of the old speech headless the flaring eyes the flaming arms the fragrant taste of bitter ambience restless to sense

...severed the tongue as if to utter if one once or could given to exile haven of dread ash the balk the rent asunderance ever

...long shadow of the abortive orifice of sun

...and echo echo from out of the filament seethe without puncture lacking in else evaporated

...echoes echoing exploratory sings of the night's accord the drag of the hours the taste of ashen tears the wilting blood

...another bone flung to the room the jaws of which are that of a pig they can bite through bone like butter

...the room devours with claustrophobe in the eye of paranoid dishevelment atrocious collapse

...this is the homestead/ grace/ the hung light evacuates

...(says '*goodnight*' to nothing of or of no-one)...

13...

My whore
my heart
I love you like we shit
Soak your ass in the storm
surrounded by lightning
The thunderbolt screws you
a madman bellows in the night
hardening like a stag
Oh death I am that stag
devoured by the dogs
Death ejaculates blood

— GEORGES BATAILLE

...corrosive blood/ axe glint in the dark

...lightning ash illumined by the arrest of sudden flash ocular

...the dogs devour the tears shed as of skin sanguine in lapse of momentary lack of resolve cast out into negate of the redempt

...hollow walled devour snap-snap cleft

...eaten of the hardening of scar tissue the erect pupil the lapse

...erectile colourings as if to say of dense kaleidoscope of burning flesh

...death marks the dawn as if to say of it that it death then other of clasp then hold prayers from shallow waters

...bellowing out no solace in

...the heart's pulse denied stricken of in the mince of grief all said undone all spoken of utter dark silenced

...the thunderbolt screws you

...'I' is the ejaculate of open the wound that cannot seal the anus of blind skies and citrus landscapes

...none else to feel and then the tumult of having broken bread with what was once to become again

...ejaculation of broken teeth seal the mouth seal the eye the eye's zero approximate

...longing then of the effect/ naught/ dissipation removal

...the other yes or no spill of intoxicative light and the break-night balm no solace from

...(hard spun lack stun mock taste shit a slash mark of desire the...)

...'I lapse'

...(sits alone in roomscape of desire/ death-death desire/ unraveling the bind)

...a bloodless pageantry/ oxide/ nothing

...(like we shit I love of the shit loved like I do not love love you)

14...

Harden old heart listen to the piercing cries
That the wounded in agony utter a long way
      off
O men lice of the earth tenacious vermin
                    — GUILLAUME APPOLINAIRE

...from tongue lapse the body bound rip lice upon given wordless corpse abounding

...intricate seasons erased as of one night of embers traces bled out morass of collapsed sudden as if to

...blood flowing from the open mouth as of benign rust hereafter cleft what sunk dredge bitten the shattered glass swallow

...spinal as of the rip agony utter old heart fresh meat upon a butcher's board

...the rain rips up the earth sky above tryst resistance of teeth no no nothing more than ever was ungiven asked of

...else washes away the wounds momentarily

...vermin laughter a glutted beast splayed for the kill man or other else-wise stun breathe

...alcoholic silences dream faculties in the else of dreaming yet bound to the liced ice famine of having to be-(in)

...bound by the step or other havoc lights and the a-dream of absenteeism shaft of black light opening up to snuff the pornography of tears

...ashen grit of teeth oceanic density closes the wound as of salt in the slit wrist bitten by lights-non-light benign focus

...colourless sky of excess the colours of oblivion lock their jaws upon the jack-knife shadow slowly passing for a being or

...design

...desire

...the reek

...dusted the eyes flat-lined as the minced heart lapsing from one grief unto the other

...(*we mock the sun*)

...spillage of clotted tenacity

...walls of warped excision the collapsed spine of haven silence echoes from out of pitch black veranda of outstretched none

...excavated vermin weight beneath the soil laughter of the blind unhearing whistles to itself alone

...the limbs are warped by the weight of

...there is blood in the eyes wipes the smile from your face

...aches as if to say

...no no not from the outset

15...

> *I can imagine the present universe being succeeded by the ridiculous absurdity that would be* UNDIFFERENTIATED BEING!
>
> *In this perspective, I consider in thought what opposes one thing to another. Nothing remains, and if I still speak, it is of the immensity of whatever is nothing...*
>
> *As I collapse, my whole being evidently collapses into this thought which is suddenly the death of all thought, the death of all being and of all thought.*
>
> *In this universal vanishing, in this failure of all possibilities, there is nothing which doesn't collapse. For ever...*
>
> *But nevertheless....A* CHINK *could remain...*
> — GEORGES BATAILLE

(*...in the present universe nothing remains ridiculous absurdity absurdities...*

...as 'I' collapses...the death of all thought...the failure of possibilities...

...a CHINK...)

...blind white of swirl degraded unto as if it were adamant sheer of the pulse in the midst of in the brevity broke snap else whittled the wilting blood amber spasm

...(*as if to murmur it were enough*)

...nothing less or more than before

...universal vanishing like the implosion of cylindrical breath in the unspeaking left or right or no hammer and tongs without motion drifting off into the kill of absolute

...in the drained white fucked no prism bell nor the collapse the mere dissipating of shadow upon shadow cancelling one another out

..."...*cut from a rarer cloth than this, I walk away, there was nothing to claim, nor keep me here...*"

...henceforth

...eye of zero zero zero wastage the echoes of which tracing the nothing of deciduous skyline spit polish

...ashen calk upon the given of or lapse

...shadows upon the tongue

...the ripped body of none as if foreign discharge of forgotten solace as if ever nostalgic spacial

...a chink

...the flesh is there the hands are there absolved in the dead weight of collapse haven of else

...evermore the laughter of silken in spite of none who's laughing now caught unawares by the speeding motor-phonic

...spews forth the distil of nothing all the same as if it were

...drowned effigies

...taste of bloodied fingers

...unspoken/ ever

16...

...praying mantis of star-lit dishevelment jackal-jackal black blade piercing the heart's marrow tide

...cut from a rarer cloth than commence diatribe of nothing spurious exile of

...white light heat of combustive solace as if clotted blood obsolete the flesh-smeared glass wiped clear

...spinal as of which declined built from the sarcophagus of tidal sputum

convex the bullet shells lie spent as shadows through obscene emptiness of the eye's disheveled pulse

...pulse yes it seeks pulse else it cannot the bind of flesh cannot be broken down dissipating like shit in a desert landscape

...asks of then of the broken lock of none spurious adroitly one footstep after the other's mark in disappearing sands

...what left or of the or/ or of the beginning of time's occluded stunt in the breath of all delivered of clasp-spun vent still else what of gathering in the whispers of

...mirrors mirrors warp beneath a skyline of extended pageantries none of which bountiful breath without end until

...until nothing ever truly claimed in the glut the swollen gut the emptiness therein pregnant the unseen knocked upon murmurs of a heart stone-dead

...clips the fingertips of the breathe known still a

barrage of cock in the midst of stone blood cunt rectum
December bone lock amber

...extracted teeth shiv by design scuttling for the
shadows once of destined to lack of none by none

cast off the heart rots swarmed by flies on some
autumnal beach stun deaf the conjestion in the skull
the in-step crack

...mean/ while of the mean-while the echo of destitute
feathers in cap not a trace of voice stammering yes
eating of the fruit the larval oxigenate

...neck snap and the spinal ejaculate

...no

...the hands fall to their sides

...unsubtle done

...the children sleep within the corpses of gutted horses

17...

...the dregs

...exigency of beyond time

...rapture of the bloodstained cloth

...one thousand bullets shear the path of one fly circling the severed limbs unsheathed

...spilled milk of/

...mock of the blind light no worship of collapsed of into the impotency of speech

...words defecating as of silenced in the parameters of gilted sugar-dusted excrement

...tide upon tide upon

...sky of or into of speckled eyelids and the breaking broke marrow crack of listless uncaring

...no nothing for tomorrow not a chance not a breath silt in the dry lungs the impoverishment of the pissoir dawn

...dugs of the earth spraying blood upon fresh meat in invisible absurdity

...the restless tears the flies will gather only martyrdom of marking it well what have you shift breath of eye spun else

...stunted shadows to reclaim with each given hour's echoing within the skull

...the eyes

...nothing to withstand

...break-neck the spinal in-between here or there
another lover loveless still yet the mark of it

...walls clawed as if to unfashion

...desire of the which that for

...silence/ the

...silence the

...unspeaking yes see if one can riddled through with
the cadaver silence of what yet will be

...the death torrent of it

...raped of the bones' faculty of it

...the skull fragments slowly beneath the

...silence/ yes

18...

I think we are in rats alley
Where the dead men lost their bones
                                    — T.S. ELIOT

...'I' think...

...rats in a barrel

...there what of never having halfed the shell the mollusc laughter

...exfoliated blood come to call upon the wilt of shadow

...exigent/ amphetamine

...echoes of from out of having been laughterling of the called upon

...brace what trace lacking still what lapse desire in effect birthing from the grave that giveth never takes away

...sun lit

...the screen blank as the eye upturned spasm lock and the breaking advance of acrid tears

...the shadow passed through the skull of benign sky feel dry rhythmic subtle as a slit throat pageantry

...(we excise in tears)

...their bones the dead men lost it cannot be replicated

...nothing of the will or cannot

...yet it cannot not a trace merely embers ashen clouds streaming nothingness from out of which one head - *petrified-* all seals unbroken

...all sound resounds through spectral tide

...cast

...words cast

...fragment of light though kaleidoscopic glass

...the dead hours where no gild doth speak

...stone a taste of iron shiv by design

...rat's alley the candelabra of the sky from pitch till pivot

...mocking the ash

...splendour of

...blind

...seethe in dry rage unblood of

...unsight of

...of broken images/ etherized upon a butcher's table

19...

The smell in here, hangs like a killer, hangs like a dead man, and I can't take another day.
— DAVID YOW (THE JESUS LIZARD-SDBJ)

...fresh meat of the unsung black light birth-ed suffocate exile

...stench room of obliterate of discarded syringes burning in a lapsing flame

...the broke bone bodies of the mind

...alcoholically spitting out the teeth from a wired jaw its seals unbroken laughter of the shadowless a-breathe

...asks yet distill hangs yes another day 'I' cannot

...fevered the collapse of entity into grave filled with children's teeth and rusty scalpels/ (as if to...)/ exhales

...the smell of you recollect/ a/ dead and the brutal flesh

...evidently hung for far too of the obsolete/ the wilting blood/ dense echo

...vibratory

...hangs like a killer unknown...

...a sinew's noose contracted the pupil grazes upon roving of the eye unsleeping in vacant lots of bound bones and acrid sentiment

...it hangs in here whispers emanate copulating shadows sprayed upon bare white walls repeat repeat again

...laughterling of pulse ocular the surrogate smear

...blood tastes like any other

...the silence weighs hangs garrotted tide of exist a swollen tongue in throat a kiss of some obscene pageantry

...'...and I can't take another day'

...they sway like the memory of nothing come to pass never engrained yet ever the return to

20...

Murky passages flow
From our eyelashes down our faces

With a fierce red-hot wire
Anger hems up our thoughts

Scissors with raised hackles
Around our unarmed words

The venomous rain of eternity
Bites us greedily

— VASKO POPA

...torso of light exigent of torso of light exigent of...

...iced walls and the dreaming of in-dreaming next of
the blood to follow on from fierce/ dead-centre

...collapsed lungs scattered to the corpsen fields till
light allay along a-breathe

...the scissor-claim makes foothold in dirt the lapse is
of what yet trace of the benign silenced effortlessly
negated

...drowned out the face of a child assailed by
butterflies their wings of razor blades unspoken of the
shadow of

...drunk destitute the wire bites into the throat
collapse of entity the 'I' in or of the unspoken of desire
unspoken

...eternity neither caresses nor

...bite wound limb a fragmented asking of in prayers bearing no religiosity

...bitter shreds to spit they poison the earth till redeem it cannot

...swallow it down thy shit in an abyss of stitches the bereft hand clasping for the essence of the shadow's drainage

...flesh dead done

...butterfly knife of intent

... the sexless waterfall of the breath exposed here now or forever after as if to say or of the erasure of speech through speech

...(is silence then the only reality, or is it the...?)

...arc of nothing within the given quarters lapse of nothing arc of bitten within the

...expired yes or no

...dreaming else

...blackened canvasses of viscid blood

...dead centre

...the approximations of none

...(till flame rescind and final/ when...)

...obsolete/ spasm lock/ expelled light/ no centre-distance

II

MEAT SEQUENCE

(AFTER FRANCIS BACON)

1

...fleshed sequence shadow meat/ once/ all at once yet
no/ nothing in shadow meat's align/ the blood calm as
untold mimicries/ by sense devoured the meat
devoured/ informed by the light which is not meat yet
of/ pageantry else yet too/ meat traces meat it is the
sun of nothing/ the sum total of nothing in/ none for
the sequential of becoming once/ in/ the totality of lack
strips emblems from meat's winds/ head stun yet other
than/ bone structures to end the sum non-total total/
swims in/ blood meat's current/ lapses no/ suffers
blind unto the white of the eye's flame it in the
reflective of/ ache lapse it is of the/ unreality of the/
meat sounds its purposeless in the night/ the un-given
of/ the dalliance is with sky/ is a jester's promise/
where only else resides...

2

...meat unto collapse/ stead lapse/ the lung's abort in
headless barrage the head is/ traces the/ meat's
sarcophagus is the light surrounding/ the forms that
bind the subject-object/ being in this from onset's
claim/ the stripping down of/   in gradual of
irreversible/ meat does not climb it cannot/ it/ blind
limit of/ in/ in conflict there its sense fed to the/ nausea
all in the face of/ the sunken eye divulged of meat/ the
meat that is the figure's construct/ gallowing from
bone/ opulent the sickness-pity for/ from unsung/
carved out of/movement through nothing the flesh/
clamouring/ cascading yet inward and then yet none/
the laughter of the meat is silent/ the its' cajole/ meat's
blood spills out of vacuum presence/ meat is not void
the head is void in conflict there the meat devoid of/
un-sound...

3

...the piss/ cum/ shit of celebratory nothing/ the ruptured meat weeps from the skin's bind/ bound upon as if it/ or/ in that/ celebratory excavations before the foot of none/ meat's saving graces in ejaculative/ voidal/ or the introspect of needle/ cunt penetrate/ rectal/ the mutilation of/ meat is the worst possible beginning-ending/ it/ other than/ the head lopped off sings to the solar anus of the eye's mind percept/ though of or or/ not from the give or the taking from of flesh/ is it/ the head is bone the body boned yet/ unto the sky there is no end it perceives the flesh null and void/ yet in the meat of the percept/ even the fault of which applies/ the whole is not correct merely because it is of the exist/ it does not burn unless it is set to/ light...

4

...object of/ scar tissue silences/ yet/ meat stings of the echo-wound/ the bound devour of in/ meat has forgotten/ the head as object desires the other it/ all stripped/ sung from the broken amulets of memory's shades of silent wasteland/ yet the meat/ still scarred/ collapses under the weight of/ consumption/ because it be/ it can yet be other/ it cannot be other than without choice/ the meat sings blood and sense yet it does not sing of final/ meat is arbitrary/ it sings in pleasure yet it does not sing aloft/ but in the expulsion of desire/ in which none is known/ terms wishes granted it/ dragging out the carcass of it into the light flaying the spectral knowledge/ the meat suffers/ it is a rabid dog in the midst of silence/ seeking to be annihilate/ yet...

5

...fleshed on in-step/ bled from/ what is it/ this/ in this
is felt yet no/ not of/ in animus of collective taste/ the
bleed of asking yet/ bound to/ the face's demolition/
the smearing of/ hence it lacking identic/ special all as
if reverberating sound in cylindrical/ yet meat's taste is
of the flesh it/ sombre ash in the guts/ in the defecate
of that already final/ as for the mock bind of sex the
interchange and shift of parameter/ meat still yet
entwined in the tint of desire's persistent edge/ all spun
together between the animal and the/ obscenely bound
to the nothing that is/ if/ where from yet in grip of
marrow beneath the flesh's desertion in/ else never
truly penetrating/ the cock lacking the hyenic bone
will/ legs splayed/ a cunt exposed/ a rectum/ skinned
the purpose of in the thrust of meat and the beckoning
void/ of it...

6

...the escape from flesh/ momentarily through flesh the
loss of being in/ subtle cataract of none/ escapade of/
the blood coming to the eyes the cum coming to the
fore/ blind-sighted/ then/ yes or no/ base flesh and the
blood-red passage through night/ in machinate of/
over again as if to/ yet never the escape from/ not
conscious deliverance nor conscious bite/ having bitten
the wick between anguish and desire/ chased by the
none of exigency and lack/ of final edge and of/ red raw
yet no/ of the blood no unless asked of/ the flayed will
reduced to ashen/ scar scar a long the indent of
emblem bitten dredge/ the frenzy of/.../all the while
the meat slowly erased/ in definite stead/ the sense of
final and over and again/ until/ bled out from circus
tint of blood/ bone lack...

7

...the Figure's lock in conditioned space/ cylindrical or no yes or no the smear/ the face obliterated/ frozen/ fleshed and death-like frozen in parameter/ shock red against the obscenity of transparent walls/ *for all time until the rot of*/ a shadow-play/ a terse/ the head divorced beyond recognition yet it bites the sky/ from a viscera of teeth exposed/ from fleshed decomposure of the gait's gouge/ swarm/ it sits it does not sit it waits/ the marrow seeping through the skin of the surface's deception/ of the what lies beneath/ all the while the movement/ the bled or blooding out of/ the ongoing that will not allow for breath/ meat tomes in shadow's trace/ matter what matter of/ but yet what wishful thinking...

8

...the bone's vibrate/ the sinew of/ placement between death and desire/ sweet death desire/ in voidal of/ scar yes or no opened up to the landscape of the meat's being/ through the excreta of silence the body never resting never silenced/ open wounds of traces forgotten never yet forgotten in the flesh-meat hung drawn quarter of a meat hook's shining/ lunged out from the it/ savoured savoured/ the pulse flower ever unseen/ the organs phantasms beneath the meat-bone structure/ bled what bled/ till/ not a fucking chance from the outset/ until the foreign of/ fleshed unto the nothing ever of the it/ now/ the blood trickles from the eyes what matter of/ smears of paint arrested colouring of vibrant bile/ of crimson shock of flesh and the bruised flesh/ all the while the scream's excavate/ the bloody lapse/ flesh without answer/ none without speech...

(ii)

('it' sequence)

1

...it/ it fathoms not/ fathoms more than previously/ it cannot quantify/ for the price of it/ after the never was of the begun/ before the less or not of it/ light slash and all the while the/ or/ it has never uttered yet/ so it says/ screams once in a while/ so it commences ever having never/ yes less than before/ it/ before the never was it can or cannot/ it fathoms not/ this/ this it or that/ what of/ what of it it will not nor ever will/ after the never was of the begun/ it has or has not it/ slides from view/ it scurries as of rat/ kiss kiss/ light extinguished/ it cannot either way/ still yet of the it it screams/ so it/ saying nothing of it it cannot/ before the less or not of it/ it lacks/ it may lack/ before the less or not of it/ it balks/ clear a lung clear a lung/ still it fathoms not it cannot/ seemingly/ what of it/ this/ merely a trace that it cannot/ still never having ever/ echos echos it/ never having ever/ this/ what this/ still it asks/ yet fathoms not/ wrenched flesh/ spittoon of blood/ was it can or cannot it before the never was of/ yes less than before it/ it/ so it says/ screams once in a while/ still it fathoms not/ light slash illumined...

2

... it/ here or there a voice it/ dense night abort/ the voice scarpers/ deceased/ nothing else/ it must wait it is said/ as if/ meaning less or no there of the/ hours of/ years of it/ it knows no bounty yet/ here or there the dissipating voice it/ scattered/ vapour lapse/ nothing else or less/ there a voice to it/ it/ scalpel/ burning/ deceased what matter then/ it cannot/ it cannot claim it/ meaningless or no there of the/ it commands nothing/ murmurs edges rot it/ lapses/ it cannot lapse/ it forgets everything that could not be recalled and hence is/ it/ says farewell too often to the rot of all/ scattered yes/ deceased no not yet/ it knows not/ knows no bounty yet as if there ever/ it/ here or there a voice it/ receding all the while it/ burning of it/ it resolves then to burn of it/ it says/ yet cannot/ there is no flame to it or of the nothing of it/ still yet of scalpel/ it commands nothing/ it cannot relapse/ it cannot lapse upon the edge of breath/ and so recalled it hence is it/ it recalls everything that could not be forgotten/ yet it knows no bounty yet/ hours of it/ years of it it cannot follow...

3

...it/ shadowing/ longing/ deft/ edge of/ subtle lock/ it/ no it does not carry on it/ vacuum else/ here another there another it/ strikes out at/ of/ wall blank face it/ shadowing/ perhaps half-light/ annihilated none/ no it does not carry on it/ it carries on it believes it does it/ vacuum other than it it does not know of/ it is bind/ bound/ it cannot/ in exile of it/ blind it carries on the given of none/ sparsely/ it cannot yet it never could/ strikes out at it/ as if it were were as if nothing was/ other than the offset/ commence half-follow breath without or of/ all spun dense as if to/ voiced from out of/ climbs/ settles in the shit of it/ the shit of it is blind/ a mark/ a signature/ wall blank face it cannot/ no it does not carry on/ choice yes/ what of it it proceeds/ avalanche/ no/ in avalanche there is no carrying on from/ it has heart apparently/ here another there another/ and the exile of it/ yes or no it/ other than it does not know of it/ yet there is/ no/ it knows that it cannot/ it beats/ yes/ absent to receive/shadowing/ long stretch of deft/ sparsely/ voiced from out of none/ strikes out at it/ a mark/ stone as of blank wall face/ it cannot/ exile of it...

4

...it/ yes it bleeds/ it cannot else it/ seeks solace in emptily/ it is not of the it cannot yet it cannot/ scar lapse of/ it cannot freed from voice it gathers speech it knows only rhythm/ roaming freely/ yes it will bleed/ the impotency of which is/ scar tissue nectar of the it of eye/ it cannot else it/ not of the it it cannot if will not/ it cannot because of which/ it extends the eye into interior wasteland/ there it cannot seek/ it has no concept of design/ it knows only the rhythm of/ it cannot else/ as if to remove itself from in the unquantifiable naught that lacks/ head of shit/ it reeks and laughs at the potency of it/ it is a nightmare of collected bones scattered at the gate/ passage through which is the price of nothing ever having been/ it scarpers for the end sign and the absence of voice/ it cannot else/ it extends the eye into the given reflex of drought/ repetition is the key that will unravel nothing/ sink the sunken eye/ yes it bleeds/ eye eye eye till absenteeism/ it cannot/ says naught/ scatters blind lock of featherings/ a nightmare collected/ head of shit/ its echoing laughter it says it does not care for context/ it vocalises the vomit chase of non-proof/ yet it knows that it/ cannot nor ever...

5

...it/ yes it will/ wills/ it will eat you alive/ wills not/ it
has or does not it will and can/ it will cease/ resend/ it
returns it will forever be/ yet no/ never was given the
benefit of lack/ in the redeem still it exists yet spits
blood from a mouth full of broken teeth/ yes it wills it
so it/ yet no remark for the it of what returns/ it bleeds
silently/ it never fully recalls/ it is a broken dam/ yet it
finds solace in the easy breeze of none/ where only it
knows and there is no/ it knows nothing of this/ cards
marked it will not listen/ it returns it will forever be of
the/ remarks upon/ passes on without motion once/ it/
yet no/ in the redeem it ceases to exist also/ given then/
something or other/ it murmurs a yes or a no/ it cannot
otherwise/ it will once again cease yet it cannot cease
of/ until/ dense then/ nothing then/ yet no remark for
the it of what flees/ silenced yes or no between the
blend of it/ without bounty/ it is yet a broken dam from
out of which seeps the/ collapse of/ feverish/ it will eat
you alive it/ it/ so it will not or of given unto wastage/
blindness/ blah blah/ it speaks it cannot speak or else/
it does not ever know...

6

...it/ eye/ what/ eye/ claim or no/ the eye dead/ the motion of it seems varicose/ spasm claim/ it dense/ it is forever other than it/ yet it/ left or right it/ layer upon layer that does not exist/ dead speeches of/ claim or no/ mark upon/ it is lashed to the edge/ it is bloodless yet depends upon it/ plays the dead speech once and over again/ says with assurance that it is all/ or/ silenced then/ naught/ none else to follow on from/ it smashes the obscure bones of nothing else to be/ or having been the nothing else of ever having/ there is nothing to it/ it could well be if the all took notice/ yet the all is of the dead speech/ hence nothing less or more/ absolute as/ left or right it will regardless mock the ember-speech nothing claimed by it/ it negates it cannot negate/ merely/ by pissing upon/ it is not the sky/ nor an open desert/ left or right/ it does not give a shit if it is incorrect/ eye/ so it is said/ it is powerless to claim/ hence doubled over in laughter it/ all spoken/ never having spoken unless/ to further on from/ what longitude/ it cannot truly negate what no longer is/ given the space or foreign of/ right or left/ eye/ it...

7

...it/ playful it/ it plays a game unto/ which cast/ dead space of/ passage unto naught irrevocable/ if it be true/ what else then/ gainful the blessed shed of eye/ voice-blind/ spun-bled/ absent of absence/ no/ it is beyond recourse/ it is a shallow dream/ yet it is/ it is not/ fragments falling/ falling fragments/ it bites vein/ it plays the game unto/ as if to say that/ if it be true/ it cannot be else/ other than/ it sieves the black/ what black no nothing of that either it/ it sieves the.../ knock knocking all the while/ a-dream in speech delivered/ hence spoken of the it is/ speaks in return/ yet it another abject/ it does not/ knocks light out with fist it/ absent of absence it/ smiles/ tokens trinkets useless all/ it can define nothing of it anymore/ it is perhaps a fault/ a fault line/ a calking of newspaper/ it a speck of/ yes/ a speck or less than/ it disappearing before the eye/ yet whole or/ yes or no it blends well/ it/ blind it yes or no it has been covered/ what/ playful it/ which cast it says/ if it be true/ it is the shallowest of dreams yes it/ it cannot live it lies to itself it/ it/ it sieves the.../in the redundancy of eye/ from out of...

8

...it/ then or not/ it in locked whisper/ less than
accountable/ it shines it cannot/ breath of/ noticed
once or twice/ exceeding/ falling/ erase it all it/ erase
it all it says/ but no the ever-clinging to/ blend of which
or will/ it speaks to the nothing of/ spit polish/ eye vast
as/ it cannot say it has no/ it speaks to it even if it
cannot hear/ all the while the ocular/ the auditory/
sense here or there and the absence of/ blacked out by
given less or less and lessening/ then or not/ between/
erase it all/ cease it can cease of course it/ on any given
day and good reason to/ it/ eye or for whatever matter/
spit/ polish/ no the ever-clinging of the/ glass heart it
is said yet/ redundant the collapse of it/ spurious none/
spurious actual light/ actual dark and the blind cliché/
of what/ echo upon echo/ cancelling out the echo of in
blind decay/ it even of the which it/ it shines it cannot
do other than or not/ erase it all/ it cannot yet say it has
been said/ dead stun/ it recedes/ it wills/ what/
nothing happens given the hours of speech have
claimed nothing/ it knows/ it does not claim to know
either/ it senses what is not/ it disregards what it
cannot else/ of...

III

GHOST-LIMB TONGUE

1

in conflict there its sense devoured/ in the wretched sting of sense/ the bite's exclamation emptily/ deduced from no worm the smite it shadows/ climbs yes or no unto pageant silenced/ asked if/ knotted breath/

not known nor of/ it tillage of deserted streets till obsolete/ in climb of emptily zones of shadow what shadowing/ seeks the naught yet the/ the naught of which that if it/ eye bites bitten lapse of the hard scar's permanence/

the wrung eye broils in silence unquantifiable/ no not of the sunlight emptily casting as upon as if it does it/ it/ all the while asking of the all what presence till/ erased for the now/ evasive interludes of knock till non-entrance silences differing from silence/

all the while the paring down/ the knotted breath of it/ the remaining pure as blood-flecked snow/ what if/ silence it was said as if/ till drought of doubt and reclamation sensed/

spat from a gouge of mouth from some upper hand/ all sense devoured/ yes or no/ from outset of there never having once recalled/ struck shine and the bitten effigy/ it cannot it is only it/ of the eye not of the/ till reclamation from the final of/ winds only/ through bone lights

2

it is a foreign feature it does not/ a-bask/ a stream of
dead vapours traces silhouettes benign smoke/ vault
none no sense of it/ exhales in turn/

in the percept of a breaking of the jawbone ground to
dust mixed with the semblance of blood what is it/
unless bled from/ directly/ piss for that matter/ the
reek of shit in actual stead/

drought doubt and the calamative axe asking of/ all
stead non-purpose of purpose worthy of none/
breathen as if to having fallen from/ till/ till closure felt
in rip of flesh a-bite/ the lock of eye that fixes upon/

dragged from the kick and scream of the machine that
claims for the intrinsic of all/ as of a bucket of rusty
blades in which to wash the scum away/ delirious tidal/
clotted laughter till hung drawn in the midst of/

it still yet not yet having recovered from the exodus of
I/ rip-blind in vacuum never yet/ kaleidoscopes of the
all encompassing nullity of/ see-saw see-see believe it
not/ it/ reduced to scratch of recoil/

in tint of black ink spilled nothing/ nothing of as of
until/ words to trace the object's surface/ the object-
subject/ irreducible no/ merely the braille of some
tangent come to failure/ grappling with the foreign
aperture/ the syringe bite/

the possibility of the other than devoid of after than/
there is nothing in the hands that reach for the throat
of doubt nothing in the hands that reach for else/ the
other/ speculative excrement/ becoming of the
stillness/ it rents no more

3

from lock un-chased/ vitriolic eye what eye/ to give of in zero complexion/ un-masked the truth of none in it/ the spasm and the lock of nothing spelled out from film of eye till glint in shadowed corner/

broken valves of feel and the abject obscure delusion/ what/ delusion of which reasoned out to climb the stairwell unto nothing ever/ the nothing of/ masked in or of/

retrace figure dead spasm figure foreign rhythm dead complexity/ eye-structure claim necessary compression of vault in-said it follows/ the emptily of till/ speak-spoken silenced final lapse/

spelled out in dissipatory/ transient waste of the trace spelled out from out of the fact/ dead-lock and the given head(less)/ I-shock/ eye/ zero point and the crack of the whip yet/

spilled blood or perhaps ejaculate/ till seasoned then all sense cast to the winds like flaked skin from the cadaver of sense devoid/ lapse and then of/ what will/ asked of/ brought to final knees of drought till maximus of silenced once again/

here now the desert ochre orchard orchid silence/ the silent knock the burrowing flagellation/ locked in/ a broken lock to a doorway leading unto utter dark/ it has been/

semblance yet it was and so it/ yet nothing of/ the sense-devoid of nothing of/ blind lock of until/ the real etched into the skin it does not matter investigative reduced to the doubt of spilled bled/

absolute devoid of/ all speech acclimatised/ pure speech merely sucks upon the dead bones of rotting sense as time obscures/ time/ what of/ the rotting sense of which/ given or taken from the hands of sense the genuflect before the/ yes or/ of what still known/ not known/

naught called into question in the spit in the eye of the square root of zero plus else/ nothing devouring the question that ever was the same/ silenced ash or/ not a trace of/ bitten till skinned of/ all purpose shredded

4

mercury light as of it/ till space misplaced untold/
mockery of harvest sheen till dressage bite long edge of
slim blade glint of eyeless trace/ dishevelled semblance
bereft of tears till flow of blood whispering of the
collapse the/

what folds in genuflect the stillness scars still felt in
drag of vibrating scars long healed/(*the sky is.../ is...*)/
absence from 'scape of lapse the longing not the asked
of given to circulate/

hence what wind to take the/ away afar the bled light
sun benign given unto nothing what it says it favours/
no not for tomorrow in break of bone whittle of pulse
the/ smoke exhaled I/

all begun from the twilight birthing given to shit/ stray
laughter and the gallows' shadow upon a moonlit wall/
says of the none it is the purity of meat/ else a banquet
for the fucking dogs of lesser wars/

from posit neutral nuclear abort *−no*/ crack/ necks
snapping goes from the what ungoing restive what/ yet
no not of the day in hand this is the/

no nothing for the words that fade cannot the gesture's
taint the promised land what fallen from asking not of
there or other than if/ no nothing the sense that binds
like else/ a snare of odds/ fragments/ vapours/

constructs from the depths of what other than non-
being/ for the/ of the/ it/ it knows nothing of it has no
place in this room of fish hooks/ fish-eyed impotency/

alacrity unto the final edge rising up to kiss the cavern
eye of roomscape opening out unto space what longing

for other than/ the/ the other than/ the story has failed
yet the words remain/

etched in unlike the/ the words fade they remain
etched in the/ the sky is not yes or no/ we betray the
sky by the maggot in the fruit of heart/ the protruding
tongue/ fuck off

5

delirium X./ barrage of shadowed clasp/ words wounds
of distant soils erased from sense context/ it is the
erased semblance scraping the shit from rat barrel rat
unto given speech what of the/

or of/ ovulation of corpse dig tend head lock what give
not ask shit stick death no none else no clap dead still/
grace of/ echo echo/ traipse skull heather in what of
knock knock sees clearer still it is blind/ it/

it clasp blind hands decide excise teeth exposed limbs
pit cum exposed cunt exposed night the night exposed/
and so as if it were from outset given unto shadowing/

across the face said once again ash across the face
blown the acrid of making nothing of the naught
endless barrage of teeth toothen well/ alizarin crimson
flesh-meat expose of/ rock stone scissors decide decide
it/

not a chance as if/ words what/ no no story silenced/
on with it said from above the incision an operating
table across which the cadaver of a woman is placed/
skin stripped bare to the open.../ yet still the indent/

what falls away falls asunder unto/ eye of lapse unto/
non-being a haven for dissent/ or/ dissent a haven for
the redeem non-existent either much or of/ spilled ink
upon exposed wound the eye's revelation of nothing/

the delirium of X. strips velvet from walls revealing the
fleshed purpose/ it perceives that it/ yet it cannot/ it/
as of/ words cast into the ever-non/ the distance of
what distance of/ ever-to-conflict with/ an un-dead
tidal of/ un-trace sarcophagus of

6

it breathes it does not.../ speaks from out of which it cannot.../ the brutality of fact –is/ it screams it cannot other than/ this is a lie as if it/ other than/

till claimed if final claims/ vertigo ice in given spasm lock of/ exhale of nothing inhaled throughout/ it/ sonorous as flesh exposed to the indifferent eye/ yet/ balm of the non-exposed/

resplendent silence ever to mock the blind stone weight of it/ fragrance to doubt/ eye to doubt/ settlement fixture/ a mess was made clean up the blood it is not/ shit-trace/ other than/ walls vibrate the claustrophobe of/

exigent taste/ where walls are blind and the taste of voice is violent/ cleaving the sense from the in/ the origin only visible in the/ the pure language is yet/ if/ it/ observed/ reliant on sense to be/

yet symbols birthed from the modern calamitive cannot be erased/...birth the outright/ the commentary/ and we all fall down into the/

it is redundant it/ likes to sing along/ along/ as if/ the repetition of dawn of the same fucking observe seals the mark the tint of breath against cold glass/ unwise and making nothing much of it/ shining down upon the nothing new/

(here an interjection here a lapse a lie a/ what speaks is the savage brutal of/ no not the lie of bankrupt/ cares not for the purity of/ divide/ divide/ splice/ obsolete/ not a fucking whisper abounding/ the fresh meat of symbols arise to cleft the eye/ divorced from/ what can only.../ be...)

7

once then from absent severance of/ it/ as if in
reclamation be/ in rooms of fresh cut grass blood-
stained cold waters/ transparent walls as of the eye's
vocality/ sensed but for a/ brutal the bone mocks
affliction meat's erasure/

there is nothing in the asking of/ the sharp ash of wind
distancing from beckon unto calling and the space
between one hollow and the next/ there or of/

walls transparent fade unto dissipating ice death-
flowering of the silk redeem the asked of nectar of
absent escape/ till seasoned less than sunlight/
beckoning none/ a shard of light evacuating bound by
the/ bound to nothing/ having illumined briefly the
nothing of/

a chalice scar and the unlocked final perhaps silence
yes or no yet from what origin/ the object lacking origin
in the simulation of the exist/ symbol yes or/ exists yes
or no it/ breathe climb it writes itself out it asks of/

no taste for the blood upon concrete surfaces between
next of conflict dream excise breath stone head sand no
head or/ bone laughterly/

laconic spread unto the flames in the ending of what
matter/ the commence of either way it/ I recollects is
what/ that I was once it is now/ viewed from an
externus-internus/ what it it cuts itself it bleeds

8

I-speech dragged out from a lapse of it/ passive cloud
rots in the eye having forgotten the day's advance/ all
sung/ breath in or out from out of glint/ where tense
and shadow do not meat/ meet/

collapse unto thy splendour I/ there will be/ stripped
of the banquet haven colour blind and sense absolved
it says/ it emptily it/ abandoned to the flex of nothing
unquantifiable/ dense words in the purity of emptily/

I cannot reach/ I has forgotten it/ there is sky in the
tide that reaches for the sky is mind where doubt forces
out the spasm/ the accumulative/ the non-
accumulative/ it negates and holds no remorse it
cannot/

blinded by speech/ the engrained word spills into the
desert of.../ spent blood upon/ within/ granular/ final/
lapsed then till the recoil from nothing nothing viewed
from an externus no winds from which/ dense flesh/

sought from seeking from/ the blood will out the crack
spill cleft dead sense no none trace when no doubt in it
it sensed it cannot be said once continuous/ we do not/
struck from the book the collective/

not a trace of it/ bankrupt/ the havoc eye tracing its
floodlights across the interior of the skull where blind
light resides to illuminate the nothing much if even/
birth/ death/ copulation/

nothing is happening here/ not a sound here/ not a
trace/ as if to garrotte the/ self what/ I what/ a jailor's
pulse to disregard the collapse of all ungiven sense
what sight to ask of in the lack malign

9

blank stare in collapse of vision replicate of final edge/
not a trace/ bled else to the surface arises a cadaver
silence it is silent/ yet silence what/ known of what/ the
sky is/ it was/ until then until it/

surface of now and again the glisten still/ stillness
pageant unlock till bait redeem taking the bait no
origin/ laughter lock of/ gathered in a collapse akin to
some velvet dreaming else/ none the non-shadowing
of/

nothing but the pulse in which of the emptily spoken/
dreams now and then wrench the meat the bone/ the
surface skin shredded by active settlements/ it no
longer tries it/ merely/

the walls yes they are there they are forever there/ till
build of nothing in the eye spit polish/ known none of/
reclamation none/ what climbs is the purity of none in
sense mocking in barrage of testament to/ done in/

blank stare reaches for ice/ the collapse imminent it/ it
is the divested of/ X.ed out I merely lapses in and out
again like a mildly corrosive element/ viewed from an
externus it cannot bite as sense bites/

yet without some sense of there would be the lack of
pure/ as if to say that/ no not the co-dependant/ unless
the parasitical be the absurdly blinding/ binding/
indent of the transient impression/

the scar tissue vomited in the midst of absence/ rock-
scissors-paper/ knocks echos as it should/ reverberates
because it can in severity of blight/ all sight non-sound/
non-being and the kick snap light blind virtue of non-
said relapse of vertigo tint until/ again

dream lapse shadowy skeletal benign clasp white sun stone dressage teeth/ itch lapse blood empty of/ no not of the collapse it then none as if to ask no place for asking of in the none it/ colours what/

vibration of and the facticity of indent/ traces out from out of sudden break from out of spill/ of further break from out of spillage terse divide/ else is a plane devoid of space yes or no it cannot collect being of the yet to come/

yet in the none of which there is no division/ absent of dichotomy/ none is the thumb-print mark upon/ the distillation breakage of subtle absent/ it is of the sense yet it is not/ it is the silent laughter of the absence of dialect/

fruition breaking against walls of foreign else/ the knocked poverty of hope begging of the lack which tomorrow will be/ else is not of the earned/ the none is the in-step into silence/ where tint is nothing and where the words form building unto step/

not the asking of nor the trace without presence/ neither the knock upon/ dream lapse is for children's bones in a mockery of teeth/ the scattered remnants ashen fragments at the feet of/ breaking no not broken yet to withstand/

all sense devoured in the eye that turns against/ not inwardly/ rationed out in terms of purpose placed/ unsung the carcass stripped of skin to reveal the meat of nothing/ where starvation does not feed/

merely observes the climate that rots away the flesh by design/ yet the senses abandoned will have their way/

even if/ if of the only to bleed resolutely from

(ii)

1

steps once/ it does not/ steps twice/ it cannot does not/
thrice in claim that cannot/ given of/ back then till
trace obliterated/ eye folds in upon it cannot echos
from out of which/ rolls in absent pageant it cannot/

of an echoing reverberate it seeks not/ no no longer
having reached it cannot/ black space open as of/ as if/
in which it/ as if it could/ not a/ no not a trace from/
lack spacious of within it opens up to graven flowering
graves of zero point/ blind edge the eye's garrotte/

dissembled/ disregard/ fingers to touch the untouch-
able/ the none untraceable yet known of/ in flesh meat
circus cavalcade/ throughout night's absurd lock of
jaw/

steps four times –*fourth*- and then retraces once again
till it cannot/ again until eye in mirror's reveal a mirror
smeared with excrement/ I cannot say/ reduced unto
absence of I/ clotted blood in specious what of it/

what is pretext of/ if/ dense/ the unreality of a cadaver
stripped of skin devouring the life from light's aborted
children/ X. + 1/ non term in relative knock what else
from which all fortitude absent/ recedes/ steps out of
view/ does it

2

bound echoes reverberate in trauma fields of scorched grass acrid shock of winds/ blood mist/ falls to knees begs for more/ as if it/ no/ stands its ground in glimmer eye and toothen sacrament/

blind-sighted allwhile no dice to ever roll from figment hand if/ if given as of foraging in transient shavings skin/ till terse devour in reclamation that cannot be it can only be if/ absurdly/

what whittles away as if embroil of plane divulged of percept and sense were some gilded key to having posessed/ erased by if/ I collects bone absently/ sets to rest in pyre of real/ moves along yet cannot/

into/ of to/ if/ sun's disease is merely paradigm/ a glaring anus/ a metaphor carries from birth and exit of/ absent lungs fill cup with phlegm/ it has seen the decay of living breathing fucking meat/

and of other than/ if/ little choice but to abscond it is said/ death nothing yes yet nothing of/ extension clause +1/ eye spits into eye that perceives it/ recollects of shadow does it/ (*something is watching the observer also*)/ yet cannot be said of/

blank space/ in dislocate/ slowly skull cracks revealing nothing that ever was/ scattered flowerings upon blood-soaked floorboards/ it was never yet nor once yet said/ if

3

psychosial whip I stings/ if clamours for shadows as if
to say that/ none silences the all of lack in purity there
absurdly   sheen   of   surface   coating   zero   eye/
unspeaking/ unseeing/

in mirror-object searching from out of indent of self
what self/ blind-sighted by cataract of percept/ it skulls
it does not it dreams in else from what origin from what
origin if/ as if to clamour/ abandoned/

a corpus of shit that is mind's resolve/ unto taken from
what matter/ doubts yes or no/ non-claim/ figment
palacial either way/ hop-scotch all said representative
erases in a deathly absence of smouldering lapse/ no
not for/

wrung neck and bloody aftermath/ skied to unrest of
absurdly taken/ back then to words that are/ if/ carried
by what into what/ in corrected present what winds to
follow/ all shine what of/

breathless   negation   suffering   up   from   collective
nothing that is within/ of speechless dislocate/ purity
of/ bitten nails and horror in brutal asking of a
facticity/ eye slashed across/ stun lock ask bitter shit
lapse stun ask lapse bitter shit if/

mock of tint in eye if eye be two/ if/ all spun together
in weave of dislocate see how they run if/ it falls
between crevice in-between give or take of what is
wished to be felt/ encore of nothing/ back then until
again of foreign purpose/ if

4

yes then or no/ commence yes yet or no not of/ blank
wall through which obscenely contraspect/ echo eye
and turn of blank to else/ block light in shock-white
emblem sarcophagus light fingers eaten away/

eye's lock closes camera lense smeared over blackened
over/ as of no redempt of it/ on with it again cease stop
all sense of which in nothing having ever/ echos white
light blank sound of broken nothing/

nothing having ever/ ever unto if/ none of in of nothing
of/ smear closed design electrical edge season spit
claim stun amber escapade reveals no not of in if or of
in else/ eye recommences centralised/

or other/ either/ either eye centralised/ again/ cannot/
basks in nothingness/ flesh + 1/ yes or no in commence
of banal(ity)/ bones thrown to empty room but one/
hyenic sense preys upon/

blank white of eye/ black slate of eye unfeeling eye
divulged of/ claims absurdly/ non-sound-non-sound/
still in echo-realm of which till trauma blunt trauma/
bitten bites down lapses/ camera lense smeared with/
if/

was once until/ no trace of which in now/ without
origin/ fleshed/ rigour mortis purpose/ fleshed bled
out/ un-sound/ in-sound/ un-seen/ nothing seen

5

eye's stillness/ screams yet/ silence/ (not a sound)/ interior echo of/ snapped what/ bone as if/ shadowy emblems/ (says the none)/

none speaks distillate it/ if/ it cannot other than/ forage closure spilled light/ mockery in or of until/ pageant rot of flesh/ actual/ being less or more than before in point of +/

one less for excavation until/ from right till left hands juggle removal eye/ replaced what nothing clamour fist/ sonorous as sky lack of sky felt if/ it/

if lack through sky be felt given to wonder of/ blank/ in lack redeem of emptily of emotive/ brutal un-sound of touch/ to touch/ walk away/ walk away commence once more/

not for amber after-glowing asking in else of/ knocks upon what space/ plentitude of silence/ irrevocable silence in exist without origin/ sound un-sound if/ no/yes/ if...

(splice-white given of/ lapse of in lack of/ spent harrow eye till claiming null...

unspeech what speech/ speech yes it/ over of or/ or/ blind-sighted/ foreign...lightless dark/ non-dark...)

6

as if/ continues next/ back-sound suck(ed) irreversible
tide once known unknown/ break/ eye folds in what
else to settle upon/ expels the mesh of speech/ travail/
distance centre-point/

skin yes there it is there/ cylindrical edge a clasp-knife
chalice/ mocks till lung abound what reverence/
reference/ density prime cut from gild what matter if/
if it is said blood's knock/ calamitous/

specious else what dark merely purity/ no nothing to
hold unto until till foreign breath's collapse/ scattered
yes or no/ blind-sighted else flowering a reek of
gardenias given up to clear sky's ember pageantry/

it says nothing it/ dust to follow onwardly unto/ travail
of amber speech claim in depth of desire unto/ non-
said it was never said it had no origin the trace
remaining merely to grit/ it is the now of the become/
it staggers unto collapse/

dense sighted in reflex of I/ eye/ bled stun/ in the
observation of the mechanics of the corpus/ distillate
un-promised from the outset never to grasp that which
is/ as if to/ blind-sung in cataract repetition/

here a proud selection of bones as of wind chimes/ sung
gladiola aptitude/ nothing no nothing more of/ bitten
lights/ the strangulation of sense weeping the sky drill
of words clamouring forth unto nothing/

from the none's testament to being in/ if/ lung what
songs for the/ cylindrical/ echo echo it returns to fill
head of bloody sands/ a deft end/ sharp struck out as
of envisage

isolate of/ cracked the frozen eye will not collect
reflection of all sung/ observed/ gouged out from out
of presence/ unto shock unto un-presence/

observing the meat sung desolate grind shock teeth
dream spurious exigent sound of which it/ follows on
through signal dense all sense devoured throughout a
passage unto absentee/

in dressage of claim upon point exact point/ what
matter/ mechanic grind of all that/ in circus affront
reveals pure nothing depth what lie/ no revert back to
from then it/

ice white is sun denuded upon peeling walls evacuated
rooms devout/ a lie a lock a lie till dense/ no passage
forth for eye/ ever the passage forth for eye/ yes or no/

sunk white emblem kiss light spasm trace eye volcanic
lapse it/strips dense meat revelation/ all said/ frozen
this or having of the not/ excises the lack in/ if other it
is of lack in/

lapse then/ yet not a trace of else/ else what matter else
in upturned eye/ graven pulse to drag/ ashen else back
through layers unto none where nothing abounds/
where nothing abounds/ where nothing abounds/

from out of which no chance no chance of escape/
welded to soil and shit a carrying of veins of earthen/
laughter bellows out of spent eye given to blindness/ it
has briefly forgotten it has not

8

excess eye non-trace trace lack origin blood-spill terse
acclimatised until/ warped walls dense sight occluded
no/ continues blank white edge of feel devour of eye
spat out unto foreign sands combed none strip sinew
breakage climb asp/

pale sun utter dark nothing of which/ shadow pulse
knock sense devour in lack from out of lack breakage
bone sight spill season tears dream/ shit/

else glimmer of hope dispelled/ eye shudders in clasp
of having perceived a blank rupture climb upon back of
breaking destitute all scars flourishing/ eye flexes
upon/ in a lack of redeem/

irredeemable naught closing fingers around throat/
spit of teeth from eye/ excessive eye/ a broken solace
inverts upon itself/ spat trace of non-trace/ eye
observes it is a fragment of glass glint in given sun
light/

vocalisation kill of dreaming lock of fathom seasoned/
utter night/ night utters as of no other/ given to speech
from out of none/

shaft shock draws down before cadaver crest/
eviscerating the vapours traces blinded/ bile chase/
dream chase/ the ever nothing/ all sight what sound

9

at close of speech/ sensed closure speech if no not from
silenced all silenced/ all/ words nothing/ non-being
what other another lack/ observes knot in veins/
intricate pulse/ as if to/ as is/ if/

it knowing yet denying the knowing unknowing/
marked tense collect/ exhausted ever if/ fragmented
blood/ endlessly night's chorus in light of sense
devouring actual/ as if to say that/ ashen nothing will
forever chalice be/

not of/ other than in glib sensed other than in else
clotted else/ hence what/ speech enclosed/ cracks glass
yet cannot free itself/ it cannot free itself/

seeks for sky/ sky remains nothing of/ absolved climbs
not from out of pit it/ abandons to/ seeks resolve in/
eye resides in mirror as much as in the observer/ flight
deals out constructs of space in-between/

over-shadowed by un-shadowed by/ else climbs walls
of forgotten exigencies/ birthed from none it cannot
other than/ static light cancels out sentence of/ words
impossible forays/

un-sight un-sound/ yet/ in vacuum of doubt's expel/
clamouring for beyond flesh what meat as if/ yet forage
no/ not a/ eye crushed within fist of none/ echoing
chamber of nothing/ never dispelled

filters out un-sound/ sound/ given to collapse into other than what once/ drained vocal of/ or teasement of until nothing ember-lock/ harsh round of echo-echoing/ a path never cleared across/

sound eclipse till given snap what stun alack/ eaten of till shadow formed across exposed eye/ non-said/ said/ from which all said all sun/ step un-step breath violet/ a glimpse of never what was ever was before/

before in asking of/ (*fade out*)/ final shiv in eye of percept/ broke bones/ sound given to retrace/ trace/ seasoned from pitch bleak lightless till given night/ in vertigo snap/ all/

sound simulations gripped by breathless/ soon to dissipate/ songs of un-being/ traceless violet songs in bloom/ distillate to point of never having been/ all purpose shredded/ white lung till breakage/

a shattered tongue frozen of inept/ in echo chamber/ steel's lament rips pulse meat flowers from given density/ on and on it/ till risen once more/ claiming that it can/ what sight what sound/ not a vulture's intricacy/

a shed of rat-black teeth in vocalise/ given to unfall unto/ bitter shards bite the eyes of sounding/ yet no lament for given loss/ white-washed wall/ stare.../

ash unlock/ blind wither claim nothing lapse/ else no treasury what nothing settled breath/ unsettled/ broke catascope undue rigour/ breaks none of lapse sequential/ sound basking in sound of/

reverberate of unknown viewed from an externus/ it/

vocalised as if to/ endless streams of sound reverberating from/ surrounding ever unknown known yes or know/ no/ if quantify/ sound bile dream ejaculate of voice/

this is sunlight it/ un-sound of which the dissipating trace/ inhaled to touch nothing/ silenced once more/ coloured by corners/ blind lights/ none abounding/ sound evacuates of its own voice/

shears black/ underwater skull/ prism promise of trace/ vapour lights/ excavuative/ echo-echo nothing/ remaining/ shutter snap down/ escapade/ wind ice tunnel of/ dense what/ sound what/

interpretive alignment/ (says what it does not know what it knows not in silent reek of inutterable bound)/ evacuates break stone blind fed none/ subtle break/ in dead as lung/ sound wither/ scattered shrapnel tines/

abandoned to silence/ still yet silences spoken of in wilt of sound/ overture of nothing claimed/ frozen in/ clasp weight lack of/ not...white ash of sound/ settling un-silenced/ silenced in/ fundamental as.../

inconclusive/ yes or no/ it posits as if to indent/ not a trace yet in blood pierces eye's unfold/ escapade lock/ stripped from out of echo/ glimpse in which/ knocks/ rejected by unseen un-sound/

nothing claimed/ not a step nor murmur/ none all stripped welcoming nothing more/ being nothing more in-sound/ yet utters what it can/

as if to parry/ it cannot/ so back then to utter blind/ light non-sound/ words terse/ no not fleshed it/ if it/ satiates nothing/ in bleed of lapse from until time/ once again...

(iii)

(the dissipating voice)

final shards

...of the echo of/ the lack/ the origin of forgotten/ the silence then unknowable/ placement of in centre dead-centre collapse/ emblems to trace/ yet never the indent...

...the ghost-limb tongue/ seeking/ to collapse the bite of silence/ ever-asking of the solace birthing/ yet never once/ nor ever/ heard from...

...yet silenced no/ never silenced/ the silence yes/ yet ever present if/ in conscious of in the reclusion from/ the empty earth's landscape/ burrowing in/ not a...

...in-step what blood/ the blood rails also yet it is
nothing/ pure tidal emptied of momentum/ desolate
ash/ the erasure of virulent laughter...

...the naught cancels out all sound/ the none is of the scream extinguished/ set to light/ consoled/ yet in the forthcoming and hence/ unconsoled...

...words no answer to/ silence unfathomable/ being's dissipation the voice/ uproots/ from depths non-existent/ films to coat/ as if to/ that coat the foraging into/ what has failed...

...evident breath and the dissipation of/ voice shed/ no words for tomorrow's foreign attributes/ the scar tissue's recession in the purity of nothing/ words clamouring for the...

...not a sound/ no/ the posit absent/ in the clear cut blood of anguish/ smeared light through which is viewed/ spoken through/ not a trace/ of...

...all broken/ fragments of stone divulged of/ scattered remnants and the misinterpretative/ the shadow's tomes of foreign where once never was/ was where one ever is and never/ yet...

...the endless night is blind/ the night is divulged of sight/ yet the eye burns of it/ zeroed out it cannot communicate through the hand's breathing/ the mind's distillate...

...dissipatory in the lack of any real substance/ either way/ here then the frozen light/ words like abandoned pissoirs/ the reek/ of decaying ice...

...and so to document the banality of/ clamouring for/ sensing that/ if present/ the defeat of the exist/ and the final etch of sight that will not/ cannot...

...voice what voice/ the clear speech of nothing ever/ the crutch of which/ the being of which it derives from nowhere/ births into the silence of the without/ the genuflect of/ silence in the/ no mark upon the...

...yet echo/ yet echo-echo/ some distance to trace/ no nothing of the distance felt it carries none into/ shadowed all the while by/ fragment/ all the while of...

...the naught cancels all/ glimmer hope and I/ else the retraced footsteps seeking outward step/ words drained in dissipate/ sands blown across erasing the tidal of...

...words what words as if to lay claims upon the nothing/ the blight of tint/ of blood flecked upon cold glass/ sought/ inconsolable/ whispers of which blind to the forgotten once/ the salient grin of/ bled out...

...yet none other than the options of/ placement between the lips/ the tide of drought and the broke bone emptily/ speech claimed till drift/ an eye for an eye's absent possibility...

...voice what words/ a mesh of/ a collective of/ none speech the purity of the last possible option/ as if to choose were to embroil/ unsought it does not ask of the other/ all the while/ fading non-relating to/ the being in/ of...

...says of the naught yet it cannot/ says of the night yet it does not/ ever yet still yet the failure of/ of retort/ not a sound/ merely traces/ projectile lights cast upon/ ever to fade out...

...still yet words empty of value strive/ in the midst of being if/ still yet the severance from/ not of the knowing of/ the what/ the ever else...

...silenced all the while in the redeem of the/ the affliction of the/ voice from out of none/ from out of the distillation *in* none/ still yet the knock upon/ never asking of the else yet it appears/ reappears...

...silhouettes of words cast off in the un-betterment of vocal/ the hands are worn/ flight is of no use where words are crisis/ crossed up/ crossing themselves out...

...nothing forever claims them/ and even yet the given term of nothing devours itself/ it cannot be believed/ it can only be a yes or no/ it is believed it...

...silence all the while scatters the dead teeth of blind obscurity/ in the exile of upon plateau a lack of defence other than in lack/ echoing out/ bleeding/ slowly out...

...echoing from out of gouge/ what gouge unto/ light what else of the other/ measure beyond nullity/ no distance/ the surface wiped clear/ not an image not a...

...sight recollects nothing/ blind speech abounds/ demarcated absent eradicated by/ silent silence spurious as the erasure of/ once spoken/ forgotten/ yes or no...

...night will forever recollect the dead in their un-
silences/ scattered films of dried bone cover no
distance/ as of snow/ the parings of the voice's
impotency...

...in dissipatory all the while/ feeding a closing space/ where the suspend collects the seeded teeth of none/ exclaims it does not/ birthed to the weight of grandeur/ the else is nothing also/ yet...

...dichotomy's bland ambiguity is an empty hand/ nothing to collect from/ the purity of none of there being it and nothing of/ spliced not/ the voice regardless buckling under the weight of in/ of in/ in this/ not a trace of...

...the silence disregards/ it cannot disregard/ so says the naught's frozen tide to shred as it shatters/ blind lack yet/ seeks out the.../ to run aground is to run aground/ no shadows' cast upon...

...in basis of/ in basic lapse/ lack/ never truly to escape silence/ regardless of the pitch of dreaming-else and the mock speech entwined with/ absences/ yet voice clamours for the/ cast tides merely in turn piss upon the reflection cast by jaded/ the jaded object...

...and so the vocal bites the tongue of dispersal/ blind illuminations decay upon their expel/ scars stretch vast into the distance having come before/ unto the basis of/ ablaze/ irrelevant/ erased/ having forgotten their origin...

...so such it/ eclipt of silence momentary/ yes or no/ silence what silence/ what/ even in deafness the vibration of sound is known/ the splice is the meat of feeding frenzy and final disappearance/ not a...

...yet still words not of this the given before which to stand/ cracking like bone fed through the machine that be/ and all of the within of it/ the here and within it/ of the/ frozen in...

gnOme is a secret press specializing in the publication of anonymous, pseudepigraphical, and apocryphal works from the past, present, and future.

"The self in no way matters. [...] He (the reader) is any one and I (the author) am also anyone. He and I, having emerged without name from . . . without name, are for this . . . without name" (GB).

gnOme is acephalic. Book sales support the authors.

GNOMEBOOKS.WORDPRESS.COM

Other titles from gnOme

A & N ● *Autophagiography*
Brian O'Blivion ● *Blackest Ever Hole*
Eva Clanculator ● *Atheologica Germanica*
M.O.N. ● *ObliviOnanisM*
Pseudo-Leopardi ● *Cantos for the Crestfallen*
Rasu-Yong Tugen, Baroness De Tristeombre ●
Songs from the Black Moon
Y.O.U. ● *How to Stay in Hell*

HWORDE
Nab Saheb and Denys X. Arbaris ● *Bergmetal:
Oro-Emblems of the Musical Beyond*
Yuu Seki ● *Serial Kitsch*
Doktor Faustroll ● *An Ephemeral Exegesis on
Crystalline Abrasions*

www.ingramcontent.com/pod-product-compliance
Lightning Source LLC
Chambersburg PA
CBHW020954030426
42339CB00005B/102